The Princess and the Bee

by Liza Charlesworth

illustrated by Kelly Kennedy

SCHOLASTIC

New York ★ Toronto ★ London ★ Auckland
Sydney ★ Mexico City ★ New Delhi ★ Hong Kong

To my
perfect pal Helen—
You will always
"bee" amazing!

ISBN 978-0-545-68634-1

12 11 10 9 8 7 6 5 4 3 2 1   14 15 16 17 18 19/0

Printed in China.

Once upon a time, there was a prince. He had a great big castle, but nobody to share it with. It was time to find a wife. There was only one rule: She had to be a real princess.

The prince rode across the land. He searched
high and low. He met a lot of girls. Some had
golden crowns. Some wore glass slippers. But,
unfortunately, none of them was a real princess.

The disappointed prince returned to his
castle all alone. That night, there was a huge
storm. *Plip, plop, crash, boom!*

Ding-dong! went the doorbell. The prince opened the door. There stood a wet girl with pretty freckles.

"Hello," she said. "I'm a princess and I'm lost. Can I stay here tonight?"

"Of course," he said kindly.

"Come sit by the fire," said the prince.
The girl talked like a real princess. She
smiled like a real princess. She even sipped
hot cocoa like a real princess.

But was she *really* a real princess? There was
only one way to find out. The prince excused
himself. He went to the kitchen and got a single
green pea.

The prince snuck up to the guest room. First, he put the pea on the girl's bed. Second, he piled 20 mattresses on top of the pea. Third, he piled 20 quilts on top of the mattresses.

Why did the prince do such a crazy thing? Because he had read in a book that only a real princess could feel an itty-bitty pea under 20 mattresses and 20 quilts.

The prince ran back downstairs.
"Time for bed." He yawned.
"Good night," said the girl.
"Sleep tight," said the prince.

But the girl did not sleep tight. Just as she put
on her pj's, a little bee buzzed into the room.

"Buzz, buzz!" said the bee.

"Shoo, shoo!" said the girl.

But the bee would not shoo. It chased the girl
around the room. It kept buzzing by her nose.
Why was it bothering her so?

Ring, ring! went the alarm clock.

"Oh no!" cried the girl. The sun was shining brightly. It was morning. And she had never even been to bed!

The girl got dressed and went downstairs for breakfast. But she could barely keep her eyes open.

"How did you sleep?" asked the prince.

"I did not sleep a wink," she replied.

The prince's eyes widened with joy.

Then she added, "You see there was this little bee."

"You must mean little *pea*," said the prince.

"No, it was a bee all right," mumbled the girl. But before she could say another word, she fell fast asleep on a pile of pancakes. *Zzzz!*

The prince frowned.

"Now I'll never know if she's a real princess or not," he said.

Then something strange happened. The little bee flew into the room and landed on the prince's shoulder.

"Psst. Forget about that pea business," it whispered. "I can prove that she is a real princess."

"You can?" said the prince hopefully.

The bee nodded. "The books have it all wrong. Not even a real princess can feel an itty-bitty pea under 20 mattresses and 20 quilts. But only a real princess has exactly 17 freckles on her cheeks. And this girl does! I buzzed around her face all night and counted them to be sure."

What great news! The prince woke up the princess. Then he pulled out a glittering ring and asked her to marry him.

"Yes," she replied dreamily.

Everyone came to their wonderful wedding.
"Hip hip hooray!" cheered the people.
"Buzz, buzz!" cheered the little bee.

The joyful couple invited the bee to become their royal pet. And they all lived—and snoozed—happily ever after!

Comprehension Boosters

1 Retell this story in your own words.

2 Why did the prince put the pea under 20 mattresses and 20 quilts?

3 Why did the bee keep buzzing near the girl's nose?

4 Does the story remind you of another famous story? Which one?

5 What happens *after* everyone lives happily ever after? Turn on your imagination and tell a story about it!